To:

From:

Date:

The Lord's Prayer for Little Ones

By Allia Zobel Nolan
Illustrations by Janet Samuel

HARVEST HOUSE PUBLISHERS

EUGENE, OREGON

For God, our Father, who has always given me my daily bread, and then some; my husband, Desmond; my grandfather, Louis Frank; and my own dear Pop-o, Alvin; for their love, support, and generous spirits.

–Allia Zobel Nolan

For Alice, with love.

–Janet Samuel

The Lord's Prayer for Little Ones

Text Copyright © 2011 by Allia Zobel Nolan
Artwork Copyright © 2011 by Janet Samuel

Published by Harvest House Publishers
Eugene, Oregon 97402
www.harvesthousepublishers.com

ISBN 978-0-7369-2662-1
Original illustrations by Janet Samuel

Design and production by Mary pat Design, Westport, Connecticut

Printed in China

11 12 13 14 15 16 17 /FC/ 10 9 8 7 6 5 4 3 2 1

For You, Little One

We have an earthly father and a heavenly Father. God is our heavenly Father, and He does everything a good daddy does. He keeps us safe. He makes sure we have food and clothes. He gives us what we need (and lots of things, like toys and games we don't need, but really want). And, best of all, He loves us and wants only good things for us. That's why He sent His Son, Jesus, to wash away our sins so that we could live forever in heaven.

When Jesus was on earth, He talked to His Father all the time. (Talking to God is called "prayer.") Jesus said we should, too. When His friends asked Jesus, "What should we say to God?" Jesus taught them this very special prayer. It's called, "The Lord's Prayer."

This book will help you learn The Lord's Prayer, understand what the words mean, and show you why it's so important. I hope this helps you stay close to your heavenly Daddy, our Father, by keeping in touch with Him every day, all through the day.

For Parents, Teachers, Grandparents, and Friends

Teaching your little ones about prayer is probably one of the most important responsibilities you have. Knowing they can "talk" to God, our Father, anytime, anywhere, about anything, will give children a sense of how much God loves them and how deeply He wants to be involved in their lives.

This book can help. It's a practical tool that explains, in simple language and child-friendly illustrations, the meaning behind the prayer Jesus Himself taught us. What's more, to make it easy for little ones to process what they've learned, I've included a "Dig Deeper" section. Use this section to encourage children to open a dialogue with you about The Lord's Prayer. Children can also use the "Words and Their Meanings" section to learn definitions of highlighted words.

Read this book often with your children and use it to bring glory to God, our heavenly Father.

Allia Zobel Nolan

Background

Have you ever seen someone **"showing off,"** or doing something so that others will point and say "Look at him!" or "Look at what she's doing!"?

Well, a long time ago, when children rode to school in chariots, some people used to **pray** not so much to praise God, but more to get attention. They would stand on the street corner and shout out their prayers so that everyone passing by would see them. "Oh, he is such a good person," people would say. "Look how he prays all the time." Other people used to pray really long prayers (it could take them hours to finish), or use big words I can't even write here because I don't know how to spell them.

But God hears all our prayers—not because we are shouting them out or because they are long, or have really big words in them, but because He loves us. So even if we pray—alone, at home—and only say, "Lord, I love You," God will listen and know we care. Jesus said, "When you pray, go into your room, close the door and pray to your Father…Then your Father, who sees what is done in secret, will reward you."*

We pray first because we love God and want to tell Him so. We also pray to **praise** God, to thank Him, to ask for help, forgiveness, or even a new toy. We can pray when we're happy, sad, afraid, **confused,** sick, or just to tell God, "Hello, I'm thinking of You." We can pray on Christmas or Groundhog Day, or any other day, at any time, anywhere.

Jesus, Himself, didn't need a special reason or **occasion** to talk to His Father. He spoke to Him all the time. What's more, He left us a special prayer to pray. It's called "The Lord's Prayer." Some people call it "The Our Father." You can find this prayer in your Bible at Matthew 6:9–13, and Luke 11:2–4. It goes like this:

*Matthew 6:6 (NIV)

Our Father which art in heaven, Hallowed be thy name.

Thy kingdom come. Thy will be done in earth, as it is in heaven.

Give us this day our daily bread.

And forgive us our debts, as we forgive our debtors.

And lead us not into temptation, but deliver us from evil:

For thine is the kingdom,

and the power, and the glory, for ever. Amen.

Let's take a closer look at this prayer and how we might say it today.

Our Father

Dear God,
Thanks for letting us call You Father.
We're so happy to be Your children.
We feel so good, we want to run, hop,
    skip, and jump.
Want to know something? You're the
    greatest Dad ever!
And we love You oh-so-very much.

which art in heaven,

8

We know You live in heaven.
But we also know You live inside
our hearts.
One day, we'll get to go to heaven.
Then we can talk face-to-face!
Maybe we can share some milk
and cookies too.

Hallowed be thy name.

Father, You are everything that's good.
And Your name, "God," is **holy** and special.
So when we pray, we praise Your name.
We tell the whole wide world:
"Our Father is the greatest!"

Thy kingdom come.

You promised us a new **kingdom.**
It will be a happy place with no tears
   or fighting.
Everyone will know You and love You.
We can't wait to see it.
We hope it will come soon.

Thy will be done in earth, as it is in heaven.

Until we get to heaven, we pray that everyone gets along.
That means no one makes fun of anyone else.
We share toys. And there are
    no wars.
That's the way it is in heaven.
We pray that on earth, we will act
    the same way.

Give us this day our daily bread.

Father, You always give us what we need.
So we pray for enough food for today.
We believe You'll give it to us because You're a **generous** Dad.
You know how to take care of Your children.
So we never have to worry.

And forgive us our debts, as we forgive our debtors.

Please **forgive** us when we're naughty.
And help us remember we should forgive others.
When someone is mean to us, then says,
   "I'm sorry," help us remember to give them
   another chance.
When we forgive like You do, we become more
   like You.

And lead us not into temptation,

Father God, we need Your help to be good.
We can't do what's right on our own.
So please lead us toward what we should do,
and **steer** us away from what we shouldn't do.
And can You please **chase** those bad thoughts
    away quickly?

but deliver us from evil:

Keep us safe from the devil.
When he tries to trick us into
    doing things that will harm us,
    chase him away.
Hear us when we call to You:
"Father, save us from the evil one."

23

For thine is the kingdom, and the power, and the glory, for ever. Amen.

God, You are our Father.
And You are also the King who
will be King forever.
Your power made the world
and keeps it running.
You've given us so much, we don't
know how to thank You.
So, we'll pray that people will come
to know You and love You.
We love You, our Father.
We really do!
Amen.

25

Digging Deeper

Now that you've read about how people used to pray, and learned all about The Lord's Prayer, let's see how much you remember. Look for the answers on the next page.

Questions:

1. True or false. God wants us to stand on the street corner and pray so everyone sees us.

2. What do we call "talking to God"?

3. What is the name of the special prayer Jesus gave us? Does it have another name?

4. Where can we find this prayer?

5. Who is "our Father"?

6. In the second line of The Lord's Prayer, we are waiting for what to come?

7. We pray for God to give us something today. What is it?

8. God forgives us when we're naughty. What does He want us to do in return?

9. We ask God to save us from someone. Who is it?

10. God is our Father, and what else is He?

Answers:

1. False. Jesus said, "When you pray, go into your room, and when you have shut your door, pray to your Father…and your Father who sees in secret will reward you openly."*

2. Talking to God is called "prayer."

3. "The Lord's Prayer" is the name of the prayer Jesus gave us. Another name for it is the "Our Father."

4. You can find this prayer in your Bible in either Matthew 6:9–13 or Luke 11:2–4.

5. Our Father is God.

6. God's kingdom.

7. Food for today.

8. Because God forgives us, He wants us to forgive others who are mean to us or who hurt us.

9. We ask God to save us from the devil.

10. God is our Father, but He is also King of the world.

*Matthew 6:6 (NKJV)

The Lord's Prayer in Dance

There are many ways to praise God. One way is through song. Another way is through dance. The dance that follows is another way to pray The Lord's Prayer. You can pray it alone or with others.

1.
Our Father

2.
which art in heaven,

3.
Hallowed be thy name.

4.
Thy kingdom come.

5.
Thy will be done

6.
in earth,

7.
as it is in heaven.

8.
Give us this day

9.
our daily bread.

10.
And forgive us our debts,

11.
as we forgive our debtors.

12.
And lead us not into temptation,

13.
but deliver us from evil:

14.
For thine is the kingdom,

15.
and the power,

16.
and the glory,

17.
for ever. Amen.

Words and Their Meanings

C
chase—to say "Go away" or send away quickly
confused—when you can't understand something

F
forgive—to say "It's okay" if someone is mean to you, then says to you, "I'm sorry. I won't do it again."

G
generous—someone who gives or shares a lot of good things with you without expecting anything back

H
holy—something that belongs to God or is about or for God

K
kingdom—the place where a king lives

O
occasion—the time or reason when something happens

10.
And forgive
us our debts,

11.
as we
forgive our debtors.

12.
And lead us not into
temptation,

13.
but deliver
us from
evil:

14.
For thine is
the kingdom,

15.
and the
power,

16.
and the
glory,

17.
for ever.
Amen.

Based on "Teaching the Lord's Prayer—A Dance Anthem," © 1999 Paul F. Bosch. Adapted from the Lift Up Your Hearts website: www.worship.ca/, with permission.

Words and Their Meanings

C
chase—to say "Go away" or send away quickly
confused—when you can't understand something

F
forgive—to say "It's okay" if someone is mean to you, then says to you, "I'm sorry. I won't do it again."

G
generous—someone who gives or shares a lot of good things with you without expecting anything back

H
holy—something that belongs to God or is about or for God

K
kingdom—the place where a king lives

O
occasion—the time or reason when something happens

P
praise—to pray or sing to God and tell Him what a loving and wonderful Father He is, or to tell everybody that God is great

S
steer—to lead someone to go a certain way
showing off—when someone does something in front of people so they will look like they are better at that something than everyone else

If you believe,
you will receive
whatever you ask for in prayer.

Matthew 21:22 NIV